The Root o

By Pastor Melba Boyd, N

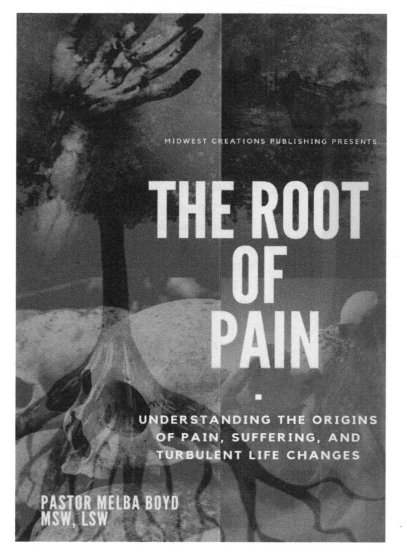

MIDWEST CREATIONS PUBLISHING PRESENTS...

THE ROOT OF PAIN

UNDERSTANDING THE ORIGINS
OF PAIN, SUFFERING, AND
TURBULENT LIFE CHANGES

PASTOR MELBA BOYD
MSW, LSW

Midwest Creations Publishing Titles

By C. Marie Evans
<u>Afro-Romance Series</u>
The Hater's Prayer
By Chantay M. James
<u>The Brainwaiver Series</u>
Waivering Minds
Waivering Lies
Waivering Winds (Novella)
<u>Other titles:</u>
Valley of Decisions
(Xulon Press, 2005)
(MWCP, 2017)
<u>Anthologies:</u>
A Hawk's Tale
(KDP) Electronic Version (MOBI)
-Author Alias: Chantay Hadley---
(*with P. Lee, D. Outlaw and A. Johnson*)
By Author Adair Rowan
Concentric Relations: Unknown Ties
By Author M. Renae
Allowed 2 Cheat: When Marriage Takes a Wrong Turn
Allowed 2 Cheat: The Study Guide
Allowed 2 Cheat: The Workbook
By Author C.M. James
Who Broke My Daughter's Alabaster Box?

The Root of Pain
Pastor Melba Boyd, MSW, LSW
Midwest Creations Publishing

Midwest Creations Publishing
Faith-Based Fiction

Midwest Creations Publishing
St. Louis, MO 63114
Visit our website at https://midwest-creations-publishing.square.site

This is a work non-fiction by the author. Names, characters, places and incidents are a may be fictional to protect the identity and privacy of those involved.

The publisher does not have any control over and does not resume responsibility for the author or any third-party (reviewers, bloggers, booksellers, social network etc.) or their content.

The Root of Pain: Understanding the Origins of Pain, Suffering and Turbulent Life Changes.

Dedication: *This BOOK is dedicated to my loving husband Earle Boyd Sr., my number one study partner. He charges me by the leading of the Holy Spirit to search the scripture. The word is the number one thing we have in common.*

Because of the word of God, we are always charged with conversation of life even after fifty-three years of marriage.

I also want to thank Doctor and Pastor Bori Oginni for his years of prayer and encouragement of myself and Rivers of Water WC Ministry in word and deed. His number one word remembered is, "Be encouraged ma'am by the Grace of God. Because of you and many other dedicated prayer and study partners throughout the years, many will be blessed."

Chapter 1

The hardest truth that we, as humans, will ever face is that grief is inevitable.

The question we must ask, ultimately, is why? Where does pain come from? Why must we go through it?

And, how do we determine how grief is affecting us and deal with it?

Let's start by listing several life-changing events that an individual might experience, some at the same time.

These events can lead to stress, grief, depression, or other dark areas that are not beneficial to believers.

Grief is not only caused by death. Several life-changing events can occur in an individual's life and cause distress. Some of these events are:

1. The death of a spouse
2. Divorce
3. Marital separation
4. Jail term
5. Death of a close family
6. Personal injury or illness
7. Marriage
8. Fired from work
9. Retirement

10. Change in the health of family member
11. Major problems with children
12. Pregnancy
13. Sex difficulties
14. Gain of a family member
15. Business re-adjustment
16. Change in financial state
17. Foreclosure of mortgage or loan
18. Family conflict
19. Change in responsibility at work
20. The death of a close friend
21. Son/daughter leaving home
22. Trouble with in-laws
23. Outstanding personal achievement
24. Began or end school
25. Change in residence
26. Change in school
27. Change in social activities
28. Change in church activities
29. Change in recreations
30. Vacation
31. Christmas
32. Change in eating habits
33. Change in sleeping habits
39. A child goes to jail
40. Change in work hours or conditions
41. Mortgage or loan
42. Spouse retires
43. Change in social activities
44. Trouble with your boss
45. Terminal illness
46. Job relocation

47. Adult children moved back home
48. Lost of a family pet
49. A child diagnosed with a terminal illness

For this exercise, circle each of the events you are experiencing right now. Give yourself (5) points for each. If your points exceed (350), you could be experiencing stress at a level that is not healthy. Why? Because hurt grows into bitterness, sorrow, depression, etcetera.

On the other hand, if you continue to read this book, it will provide steps toward acquiring the tools you need to resolve the hurt or grief you may be experiencing.

Chapter 2

Looking at the Root of Pain

Where did it begin? Certainly not with man individually. The pain started when Adam and Eve gave more attention to what Satan said than what God said.

In Genesis 2:16 – The scripture says, "...and the Lord God commanded the man, saying, you may freely eat of every tree of the garden; "

Genesis 2:17 "...but of the tree of the knowledge of good and evil and blessing and calamity you shall not eat, for the day that you eat of it you shall surely die. "

God never intended for man to have pain, die, or to be spiritually separated from Him. God never intended for Adam to know evil. His intent was for their relationship – fellowship to never break.

Verse (25) says, "...and the man and his wife were both naked and were not embarrassed or ashamed of each other's presence." (Shame and embarrassment is a form of pain)

Genesis 3:6" And when the woman saw that the tree was good for food and that it was good to look at and a tree to be desired in order to make one wise, she took of its fruit and ate; and she gave some also to her husband, and he did eat." (AMP – Amplified Bible)

Genesis 3:7 "Then the eyes of them both were opened, and they knew that they were naked, and they sewed fig leaves together and made themselves apron like girdles." (AMP – Amplified Bible)

Adam and Eve never knew pain, shame, sorrow, toil or fear until he disobeyed God. Why? Because Adam did not know evil.

Genesis 3: 9 and 10: "But the Lord God called to Adam and said to him, where are you? He said, I heard the sound of you walking in the garden, and I was afraid because I was naked, I hid myself."

The Lord was not there to punish Adam; he was there to fellowship with him as usual.

Look at the pain that came with disobedience and separation from God.

Genesis 3: 16: The Lord said to the woman, I will greatly multiply your grief and your suffering."

Genesis 3:17 "And to Adam He said the ground is under a curse because of you: in sorrow and toil shall you eat of the fruits of it all the days of your life."

God knew that Adam would make that choice.

God knew that it was impossible for Adam to follow his instructions without His supernatural support. God already had another plan in place to rescue man. God's plan was that man not suffer eternal damnation even though man chose to put himself in that position. Not just Adam, but mankind. At this point, Adam had not realized that he could not accomplish living a perfect life in a perfect environment independent of the Spirit of God.

It is the Spirit of God that gives man his unlimited ability to endure, believe, and have hope.

Genesis 3:24 Notice the scripture say, so (God) drove out the man; and He placed at the east of the Garden of Eden the "cherubim and a flaming sword which turned every way, to keep and guard the way to the tree of life. "

If man had not been driven out of the garden, sin-pain-evil would have been eternal.

Once during a support group session, I had a lady (let's call her Rose) request to tell the story of the death of her spouse. Rose stated she and her spouse basically enjoyed life.

"We only had one habit that was not good for either of us. We enjoyed sitting on our outside patio smoking and drinking iced tea or coffee every morning and every evening."

Rose went on to explain that how over time, her spouse was diagnosed with poor circulation.

"First, they amputed his foot. Less than a year later, he had to have his leg amputated above the knee. The doctor counseled us and strongly suggested my husband stop smoking. Instead of following the doctor's request, we continued to enjoy our time doing the same thing we'd always done."

Tears fell as Rose confessed that, had *she* stopped smoking, maybe her support would have been what her husband needed, and he would be alive today.

Clearly Rose has continued to experience emotional pain, including grief. Not only that, but she was looking at her past, thus hindering her future. Her spouse had been deceased for over five years. Rose has since remarried yet she is still experiencing recurrences of pain that have not ended.

Some years later, I saw Rose in Walmart as I entered the store. She was working, welcoming customers in the store. She stopped me to share that she and her current spouse are attending church together.

I was happy to hear that, with group counseling, she found others in the group that were having similar experiences.

"My previous husband isn't here to forgive me. I now know that I had to forgive myself and move on."

Rose then shared a scripture that her pastor had given her to meditate on. It was Romans 8:1 which advised that there is now no condemnation (judging as guilty of wrong) for those who are in Christ Jesus – who are those that no longer live after the dictates of the flesh, but after the dictates of the Spirit." (paraphrase).

"I no longer allow the past to control my future," Rose finished, "which has made a big difference in my new marriage!"

Chapter 3

Nobody knows how I feel...

As a pastor and social worker, I have counseled many that say, "People just don't know how bad I am hurting."
That might be true.
Some people are grieving, broken-hearted, or maybe at that very moment, experiencing the death of a loved one.
I have even had some express that they are experiencing "all of the above" at the same time.
These hurting individuals often begin with, "I don't even know where to start."
I recently provided service for a lady (we will call her Sandy) who felt isolated because most close family members on both sides were deceased, the lone exception being a son.
Sandy shared, "My husband and I worked hard all our lives. After the children moved away and were living their own lives, we decided to do some traveling and just enjoy life. On our second trip, my husband became critically ill.
The doctor informed me that he had lung cancer with limited life expectancy."
Her brokenness apparent, Sandy explained how her husband was

discharged from the hospital to their home with twenty-four-hour care needs until he died.

"As I was recovering from the shock, I was thankful that our son could visit more and help me with caring for his father. It worked out to the extent that we both had another opportunity to bond with our son healthily."

I sighed in relief at the thought of something good coming out of this experience for her, only Sandy wasn't finished.

"It was during the time that I continued to provide care for my husband that I noticed my eyesight deteriorating."

The doctor informed Sandy that diabetes was causing the loss of her vision.

Sandy, as we discussed prior, was having two grief experiences at one time. She was losing her husband and, due to her health, her eyesight as well.

How do you cope when unexpected grief occurs? As believers, we must depend on the word of God like Rose did. Despite how bleak things look in the moment, we have to believe that weeping may endure for the night, but somehow, someway... joy WILL come in the morning.

***

I'm devastated: Severe and overwhelming shock or grief...

Let's go back to the beginning of how I'd originally met Sandy.

I'd received a referral as a Social Worker to help with community resource planning and socialization options in the surrounding areas.

Upon arrival, I introduced myself to Sandy who immediately explained that her doctor had made her aware of the reason for my visit.

Sandy acknowledged that she was aware that her doctor was sending me, her eyes narrowing as she explained,

"I told him there was nothing anybody could do for me! You can't expect me to leave my husband in the hands of someone else."

I suggested, "I understand how you feel. But maybe this respite time might be what you need to help reduce your level of stress?"

"How's that? You know I can't drive, right?"

In that moment, I realized what she meant. Her thought was not just about the time that she would have to leave her husband alone; it was also having to depend on transportation from strangers that further complicated her situation.

As this dawned on me, Sandy yelled, "Lady, I don't know why you think you can make things any better for me! I know the doctor thought it would help but..."

We talked a bit more, calming her down during that time.

Finally, Sandy thanked me for coming adding that this was just not a good time or day for a visit.

I agreed with her feelings and told her that she could schedule another date when she was up to it. I spoke more comforting words as she walked me to the door.

I wish I could say that Sandy's life got better from there. Sadly, sometimes that just isn't how life works.

***

I can't take it anymore!!!

To my surprise, about a month later, the nurse who was still on Sandy's case suggested to me that since we'd met, she'd had other losses.

The nurse explained how Sandy may be grieving and/or showing signs of depression. When I called to arrange another visit with her, Sandy remembered me and accepted.

When I arrived this time, she invited me in but did not speak for a while. We both sat in silence until she was ready to talk. Then she began to cry. Finally, she started telling me about her son, whom I thought continued to be her primary family contact.

Sandy appeared to continue experiencing trauma from an incident that took place in her home.

"My son came through that door at least three days a week during his dad's illness. He was always joyful and full of jokes and laughter. He set the atmosphere for a relaxed evening, even though his dad was ill. And he kept our refrigerator full of food. He was my rock."

Until six months ago.

My heart broke for her as she explained what happened then...

"...he came through the door and fell to the floor, not saying a word. And that's where he died."

Sandy had found out later that her son had been sick himself but hadn't told anyone. That night, he'd had a massive heart attack, and now every time she looked toward her door, she relived losing her son over and over again.

"I'm alone in this house, and I can't face taking the next step. It's too hard! For a while, people came around to support me, but more often than not, I find myself alone. The crying spells just won't go away, and the pain is beyond any expression of words. I have friends, but right now, I have no interest in being with other people."

Sandy had thoughts that maybe her life had no value.

It is during times like this that we should turn to the thoughts that are higher than ours. As believers, we must depend on God's thoughts toward us to get us through terrible times like these. And those who love us.

The times when you want to be around people the least, may be the times that you need them the most.

Chapter 4

Self-Judgement – A strong emotion...

My concern for Sandy growing by the second, I asked her if she has fellowshipped with a church in the past?

She reminded me that she has had no transportation since the loss of her eyesight and her son.

"I'd probably feel uncomfortable attending church right now, anyway."

I silently mourned with her as I mentally consulted my comforter for words that would help.

"What have I done to deserve all of this?"

The answer, of course, was nothing. I stayed silent. Then she continued, "Sometimes, I think I have lost it!"

Finally finding the words I needed to help her through this, we began our talk.

We discussed grief as a normal reaction to her loss; her multiple losses. With the appropriate support system in place, Sandy could work through each loss, one at a time.

As a Christian, Sandy had many questions about the word of God.

She recalled the scripture in Isaiah 53:3 that discussed how He was despised and rejected, a man of sorrow, acquainted with deepest grief. (paraphrase)

"I think Jesus knows how I feel," Sandy finished, dejectedly.

***

Going back to our explanation of the root of pain, God never intended for man to experience such devastation; however, because of Adam's sin, the curse came upon all; Jesus came as the solution to break the curse of sin and death.

Hebrews 4:14 reads "So then we have a great High Priest who has entered heaven. Jesus, the son of God, let us hold firmly what we believe. This High Priest understands our weaknesses, for he faced all of the same testings we do, yet he did not sin. So, let us come boldly to the throne of our gracious God. There we will receive his mercy, and we will find grace to help us when we need it the most." (NLT - New Living Translation)

Grace is God's power and ability working in you doing for you that which you cannot do on your own.

Sandy needed God's help.

After discussing these truths, she cried out, "Lord, I need your help!"

Romans 5:8 further explains, "But God showed his great love for us by sending Christ to die for us while we were still sinners."

Romans 5:9 continues, "And since we have been made right in God's sight by the blood of Christ, he will certainly save us from God's condemnation. "(NLT- New Living Translation)

Last, Romans 5:19 quotes, "For just as by one man's disobedience all were constituted sinners, so by one Man's obedience all will be constituted righteous (made acceptable to God, brought into right standing with Him) "

Through the obedience of Jesus Christ, all who believe now have an opportunity to experience the benefits of the righteousness of God!

Righteousness, as the scripture declares below, is a free gift to us from God.

"...just as sin has reigned in death (so) grace (His unearned and undeserved favor) might reign also through righteousness (right standing with God which issues eternal life through Jesus Christ (the Messiah, the Anointed One) our Lord." Romans 5:21 (AMP – Amplified Bible).

Chapter 5

You are FORGIVEN, not judged!

Instead of entertaining the thought that you have done something wrong, it is okay to acknowledge that Jesus did everything right on your behalf.

Eternal life includes salvation, forgiveness, prosperity and healing. In other words, if you are a child of God through faith in Jesus Christ, your sins- today- yesterday, and forever have already been forgiven. We are not being judged because of sin.

John 3:17 tells us that God did not send the Son (Jesus) into the world to judge (reject, condemn, or to pass sentence on it, but that the world might find salvation and be made safe and sound through Him. (paraphrase).

So again, that lets us know that this is not the dispensation of judgement. Judgment brings with it guilt, condemnation, fear, anger and so much more.

Know that whatever pain you are experiencing right now, it did not come from God. **For God is love.**

1st John 4:18 says, "There is no fear in love; but perfect love casteth out fear:

because fear hath torment. He that feareth is not made perfect in love."

2nd Timothy 1:7 declares, "For God did not give us a spirit of timidity (of cowardice, of craven and cringing and fawning fear), but [He has given us a spirit] of power and of love and of calm and well-balanced mind and discipline and self-control." (AMP – Amplified Bible).

In John 10:10-11 Jesus said it this way, "A thief (Satan) only comes to steal-kill-and destroy." Jesus said I came that you might have real and eternal life. "I am the Good Shepherd. The good shepherd sacrifices his life for the sheep."

John 3:17, "God did not send his Son into the world to condemn the world, but to save the world through Him."

***

Dealing with Negative Actions, Emotions, and Thoughts...

Escalation of pain means that we have to take control and rule over our thought life.

Let's go back to the beginning of creation where, in Genesis 1:26 it says, "Then God said, "Let us make man in our image, in our likeness, and let them rule..." (NASB – New American Standard Bible)

God created man in His own image without evil or pain. And to rule. Ruling starts with our very selves.

Genesis 1:28 further explains that, "God blessed them (Adam-Eve) and said to them be fruitful, multiply, and replenish the earth, and subdue it; and have dominion." (AMP – Amplified Bible)

Verse 31 keeps this going, indicating, that everything God created was good, including Man (paraphrase).

Good means no evil or pain. There is only ONE emotion in operation eternally and that emotion is the love of God.

Because God loved man, He made all provision for man to live a life without struggle.

In Genesis chapter two we learn that God instructed Adam to dress and keep the garden. We read on and learn that God had told man he could eat of very tree in the garden except the tree of good and evil because God knew that evil would bring separation between God and man.

Before Adam made the choice to eat from the tree of good and evil, everything was good.

The plan of God was for man to live without evil.

Satan knew that Eve did not receive direct instruction from God, as Adam did. Eve made the decision to respond to Satan out of her five senses.

The scripture says, she saw the tree, desired, ate. Everything was positive before Eve's decision to eat from the tree of good and evil.

However, we know that deception was not a positive act. Nor did it generate positive emotions. Its effect was quite the opposite.

Once their eyes were open to good and evil, the mind and soul began experiencing those negative emotions. It was like a domino effect, one evil resulted in another.

As we continue to follow the scripture, we find that Jesus would be the only remedy for pain and evil, something God never wanted man to experience in the first place.

Know that when you are under attack, it always comes as a thought <u>first</u>.

When it comes to negative thoughts, the voice of Satan will attempt to speak to your natural mind.

There are three voices that may speak to you. Yours, Satan's and the Lord's, if you are a believer.

If you do not believe in Jesus Christ as the son of God who died for your sins and rose from the dead with all power and authority, then you will not recognize the voice of God when He encourages you to choose the positive.

Jesus said, "My sheep know my voice. They hear me and another voice they will not follow."

Abraham, speaking as an authority, declared that before the people God sets the choice of life or death (positive or negative), blessing and curses, and to CHOOSE LIFE that you and your descendants may live." (paraphrase)

Nobody really wants to choose death or a curse on themselves; to do so would cancel out God's blessings.

The emotions experienced before man's sin had been all positive. Genesis 3:6 tells us that Eve was tempted of the good thing that she thought they might experience by eating the fruit from the tree of good and evil. (paraphrase)

The nature (natural) mind that has not been transformed by God's word tends to live by its senses: things you can touch, feel, see, hear, and taste.

If that were truly our limitations, any of us could fall into the same trap as Eve.

After their fall, when God called man, Adam experienced the negative emotion of fear, and because he was afraid, he hid himself.

Adam knew he'd made the wrong choice by disobeying God. In that moment, he began experiencing one negative emotion after another.

Genesis 3:17 provides insight into the emotion of sorrow that they suffered, and how it would become a lifetime experience.

This further proves the point that God never intended for man to experience negative emotions.

Since Adam opened that door, he suffered the consequences. And we see that in the scriptures following.

"The Lord God said, 'Behold man is become as one knowing good and evil; and now, lest he put forth his hand, and take also the tree of life, and eat, and live forever. The Lord banished Adam from the Garden of Eden and placed on the east side of the garden cherubim and a flaming sword to guard the way to the tree of life so that man would not receive eternal damnation." (Genesis 3:22-24)

God loves us so much. He did not allow the option of eternal damnation unless it was man's choice/decision.

If you are one who is not sure of your salvation, you can invite Jesus Christ into your life.

John 3:16 tells us that God so loved the world that He gave His only begotten son, that whosoever believeth in him shall not perish, but shall have everlasting life.

In other words, through Adam, the punishment of death came to all God's creation. Jesus paid the price for death/judgement through His death.

Those who believe have been given the abundance of grace, the gift of righteousness, and the power and ability to reign in life by one, Jesus Christ. To reign means, like Jesus, we don't allow negative emotions to control our lives.

God has given us His power and authority to control and His grace (ability) to direct the force of our emotions, and that does not mean we become emotionless.

That does not mean to withdraw or decide that you will suppress your feelings. God created us with emotions to enjoy.

1st John 4:8 reads, "Anyone who does not love does not know God, for God is love. "(NIV)

God himself is a God of emotion.

Chapter 6

Don't listen to Satan...

He does NOT tell you the truth.

Notice how earlier in Genesis the scripture points out that Satan, the serpent, was more clever and crafty than any living creation of the field which the Lord God made?

We find him in Genesis 3:1 *craftily* speaking to the woman.

"Satan said to the woman, can it really be that God has said, you shall not eat from every tree of the garden?"

Know that when you are under attack, it always comes as a thought first.

The voice of Satan will speak to your natural mind.

Satan says things like, "You're going through all these trials because God is punishing you!"

Or, "...you did something to deserve this! God is angry at you!"

To better illustrate this, let's jump to a different book in the Bible for a minute. In the book of Job, you find a man suffering from several of these grief events we talked about. All at the same time!

Hurt, suffering and under a great deal of emotional stress, while he didn't "curse God and die," as his wife suggested, he did make a few rash and emotional statements.

Thus, we find him in Chapter 42 verse three saying, "I have rashly uttered what I did not understand. "(paraphrase)

In other words, in the beginning, when Job lost everything, including his family, he thought he was being judged or punished by God.

Many of us have felt this way too, at one time or another.

When we experience life-changing situations or what the Bible calls "the cares of the world," it is essential that we know the truth about pain instead of listening to Satan's lies.

Hebrews 13:9 talks about how it is a good thing that the heart be established by grace and not to be deceived with empty words. Strong's Exhaustive Concordance links "a heart established by grace" to "the word of truth" in, for example, 1 Timothy 2:15, as a reference to Paul's tendency to use different words that express the same truth.

Thereby "the heart established by grace that is not deceived", is the same heart that allows a workman to handle God's word of truth diligently, not being deceived or, mishandling it himself.

We cannot allow the lies of our enemy to confuse us into believing that our troubles can destroy or overcome us or that they are sent by God each time we experience suffering.

Jesus said himself in John 16:33 (NIV) "I have told you these things, so that in me you may have peace. In this world, you will have trouble, But take heart! I have overcome the world."

2nd Peter 1:4 mentions how we have been given exceedingly great and precious promises, and through them we would be partakers of God's divine nature (through Christ Jesus), having escaped the corruption that is in the world through the lusts of men. (paraphrase)

That means that Satan lies! And his lies ought to have no power over us.

Chapter 7

Escape Corruption...

It doesn't seem possible, does it?

Naturally thinking, it just isn't realistic that one could escape the corruption of this world. It certainly does not agree with man's five senses, anyway.

In 1st Corinthians we find help in understanding this.

Chapter 2, verse 4 reads, "The natural man does not accept the things that come from the Spirit of God, for they are foolishness to him, and he cannot understand them, because they are spiritually discerned." (AMP)

Escaping corruption on our own may be beyond us. Luckily, we are not alone.

Knowledge in the heart of a believer of what Jesus has spoken will allow them to uproot negative thoughts and partake of Jesus' divine nature. Instead of painful and corrupt thoughts, we get to enjoy living in His promises of hope and peace.

So, when we spoke earlier in the last chapter about a "heart established by grace," or in clearer terms, "a heart established by the word of Truth," we must ask the question, "Why does knowledge need to be in the heart?

Luke 6:45 teaches us that, "A good man brings good things out of the good stored up in his heart, and the evil man brings evil things out of the evil stored up in his heart. For the mouth speaks what the heart is full of. " (NIV)

Constantly talking about the circumstance that caused pain or suffering leads to a deposit of negative seeds in the heart.

Negative seeds become negative thoughts.

Negative thoughts make the heart sick! For example, let's look at a very real situation that can allow a negative circumstance to consume your thought process.

Once during a group session, one of the members (we'll call her Pam) talked about her 2-year-old granddaughter's death.

Pam discussed how she accidentally backed her car over the child, killing her; mistakenly believing her grandchild was in the house with a family member.

Heading to the store for her daughter, Pam had been completely unaware that the toddler had followed her out the door.

And because there were always toys in the drive way, having no idea the child was outside, upon backing her car out Pam thought she'd missed removing one of the toys. Immediately, she drove the car forward to remove the toy. That was when she saw the child lying there. She screamed as she picked up the baby, calling out to her daughter hysterically. They called 911.

Fearing the worst, they didn't wait for first responders. Pam drove the child to the hospital, her mother holding her tight. Pam's granddaughter took her last breath in her mother's arms.

Devastated and heartbroken, Pam could not get the thought of the incident out of her mind. Worse yet, she kept reliving the incident.

It's been several years since her daughter and other family members have spoken to her. Even when her husband died while on hospice, none of the family members supported her.

In all of that, Pam added that this was the worst part:

"I don't think they ever forgave me, and I'm having a hard time forgiving myself."

It was hard to know what to say, not just in this circumstance but in any situation where this level of pain is experienced.

Pain is pain, including the emotional kind. Isaiah prophesied the solution for pain would come through Jesus Christ.

"For to us a child is born. To us a son is given, and the government will rest on his shoulders. And he will be called: Wonderful Counselor, Mighty God, Everlasting Father, Prince of peace." Isaiah 9:6 (NIV)

In other words, Jesus' Spirit abides in the believer to counsel him. The Holy Spirit reminds the believer that he has peace, which is a gift from God.

"You will guard him and keep him in perfect and constant peace whose mind is stayed on you because he commits himself to you, leans on you, and hopes confidently in you." Isaiah 26:3 (AMP)

In other words, although you are having an uncomfortable experience, lean on and trust in your comforter. He will get you through. You will experience his inner comfort.

With all Pam had been through, matters worsened within a year when her husband was placed in hospice care. He had been in the nursing home for some months when she lost her job due to multiple nervous breakdowns.

With looming bills at the nursing home and no income, she eventually lost her home. Pam had no family support partly due to un-forgiveness related to her grandchild's death. Pam's daughter had informed her that she could never forgive her for killing her daughter.

Pam believed Satan's lies, lies that convinced her she was being punished for that incident.

She was experiencing multiple life-changing events that were not in her control. Pam expressed thoughts of suicide and began speaking to a psychiatrist who prescribed medication.

Despite being a regular in a grief support group and a Christian, Pam felt that she had no worth. Her mind was in constant torment. Torment is a key indication that someone is listening to the voice of Satan.

While Pam's story is truly heartbreaking, a believer should always have hope. Unfortunately, Pam was lost. It was as if she couldn't bear the pain of one more thing going wrong in her life. It appeared that she just could not see herself moving from this type of pain to a normal life again. Thoughts of truth slipped away slowly even though, as a believer, she had control of her own heart.

Believers can be reminded of scriptures of meditation that can help them maintain self-control.

Philippians 4:8 (AMP) says even in our worse moment,

"Whatever is true, whatever is worthy of reverence and is honorable and a seemly, whatever is pure, whatever is lovely, and lovable, whatever is kind and winsome and gracious, if there is any virtue and excellence, if there is anything worthy of praise, think on and weigh and take account of these things (fix your minds on them) pure, lovely, kind, worthy of reverence, just, worthy of praise, of a good report think on these things. "

Satan brings terrible imaginations to the natural mind. He tells us we are the worst and no good to ourselves or anyone else.

Think about that.

He's crafty, remember? He comes to you when you're already feeling bad.

2 Corinthians 10:5 tells us how we can destroy arguments and every proud obstacle to the knowledge of God, and take every thought captive into obedience to Christ Jesus (paraphrase).

This scripture can only be fulfilled in a believer's life if the word of God is established in their heart.

Once the negative seeds are planted in the heart, a believer battles in what the bible calls "spiritual warfare".

That simply means the soul (mind, will, and emotions) are at war with your spirit.

The pain Satan introduced to Eve is the same pain he introduces to all believers today.

1 Peter 5:8 puts it this way: "Be sober, be vigilant because your adversary the devil, as a roaring lion, walketh about, seeking whom he may devour. "

The devil is out to destroy lives. Pain is one of his inroads to doing exactly that.

To combat that, we have what Galatians 5:22 describes as "the fruits of the spirit".

If you are experiencing pain (cares of this world), whether physical, emotional, mental, or spiritual, due to life-changing events, that's called a spiritual battle. All spiritual battles were actually won through the sacrifice of Jesus Christ on the cross.

In John 16:33 Jesus said, "In me, you have perfect peace and confidence. In today's world, you will have tribulation, trials, distresses, and frustration; but be of good cheer as I have overcome the world." (paraphrase)

Jesus overcame every spiritual battle that man would experience in a lifetime.

He knew that Satan would attack our natural mind with a spirit of grief, depression, guilt, shame, and so much more. He allowed Satan to flood his mind with all of the above so that he could gain our victory.

When Satan came against his mind, he spoke victory according to Matthew 4:4,

"Man does not live by bread alone but by every word that proceeds out of the mouth of God."

Remember, as explained earlier, every battle we experience happens in the mind first.

Satan has no control over you, nor can he defeat the people of God through demonic force. We can speak the same truth that Jesus spoke when he was under attack from Satan.

In Philippians 2:5 Paul declares, "Let this mind be in you that is also in Christ Jesus."

That scripture is talking about the mind of the Spirit. The mind of the soul can open the door for defeat in the life of the people of God through thoughts.

The answer that will defeat the power of the enemy is found in scripture. Our responsibility is to change the way we think through knowledge of the word of God.

Romans 12:2 says, "Don't be conformed to the world's way of thinking but be transformed by the renewing of your mind."

While Isaiah 54:17 tells us that, "No weapon formed against you shall prosper..."

So again, don't listen to the deception of Satan who might say you are being punished; that you've done something wrong and that God is angry at you. One of the reasons that Jesus came is to heal you wherever there is pain.

When God asked Adam, in Genesis 3:9 "Where are you...," He was there to fellowship with Adam as He'd done many times before.

Adam imagined that God was there to punish him. His mind was warring with vain imaginations that came from the flesh.

In the scripture Galatians 5:24, the Apostle Paul said, "If you belong to Christ, the passions of our sinful nature have been crucified with Christ."

2nd Corinthians 10:5 tells us how we ought to "cast down imaginations, and every high thing that exalts itself against the knowledge of God."

In other words, any thought that is not consistent with the knowledge of God is a vain imagination.

This scripture says we have the power and ability to bring every thought into obedience to Christ, knowing that Satan has no power over us. He, nor any other person, can judge you or attempt to make you feel guilty for anything that happened in your past.

There is no guilt or condemnation to those who are in Christ (belong to Christ).

You must decide in your heart not to listen to Satan. He is subject to the name of Jesus. Peace and joy have been given to us as believers through Jesus Christ if we believe in our hearts.

Chapter 8

Only one can understand...

As I mentioned earlier, I am both a Pastor and a counselor.

That said, I have had several opportunities to counsel and help others through grieving, broken heartedness, dying or experiencing life-changing events.

Some talk about their fears, families, successes, failures, problems, regrets, pain, and unfinished business. I am often told, "Nobody understands what I am going through nor how I feel."

Remember Sandy's story from before, how after becoming empty nesters she and her husband decided to travel? Only to find out that he was gravely ill, followed by which she began losing her sight, her sadness culminating with the sudden death of her son? Remember when she yelled out, "I can't take anymore!" and "No one understands how I feel?"

There is only one that *can* truly understand our deepest hurts and the grief we suffer.

Often the pain is beyond the expression of words. No other human indeed knows the deep ache experienced in our hearts.

People who love us try to say the right words. Those that care would give anything if they knew what would console us, but deep in our hearts, we know they can't comfort us. Other people just don't really know what we feel and what we need.

Sometimes in life, it feels like we are going from one hard place to another; however, there is a spiritual reality.

Hebrews 4:15 teaches us, "For we have not a high priest which cannot be touched with the feelings of our infirmities but was in all points tempted like as we are, yet without sin."

In other words, Jesus suffered pain, physically, mentally, and emotionally on behalf of mankind, whom he loves and for whom he gave his life.

His purpose was to take on man's frustrations, guilt, pain, and suffering for an exchange of hope.

In these situations, we have a choice to make.

We can choose to live in fear. Or we can choose to live in faith.

Think about it; if you are struggling to get through situations grasping for answers, fear will be there waiting on you to make a choice.

That's the perfect time to meditate on the written word of God.

Psalms 27:1 counsels that, "the Lord is my light and my salvation, whom shall I fear?..."

2nd Timothy 1:7 adds to this, "For God hath not given us the spirit of fear, but of power, and of love, and of a sound mind."

Did you notice that the bible talks about a spirit of fear?

Let's just look at the scripture in Romans 8:10 -11.

"And if the Spirit of Him who raised Jesus from the dead is living in you, He who raised Christ from the dead will also give life to your mortal bodies because of His same spirit who lives in you."

Through the Spirit of Jesus Christ, the power to believe what He has spoken is ours.

Remember, fear started in the Garden of Eden after the fall of Adam.

Jesus announced to all that He came to give us life in abundance!

Sometimes we feel God just forgets us amid our hurts and pain, but this is a lie from the devil.

Jesus is the one person who understands how we feel. We can trust Him with our physical, emotional, mental, and spiritual concerns.

In Isaiah 26:3, God advises us that He will guard us and keep us in perfect and constant peace, provided we keep our minds stayed on Him. (paraphrase)

Don't wait until hurt, pain, or some type of devastating situation occurs in your life. Start believing and trusting in God now.

Chapter 9

There is no pain in a believer's Spirit...

Pain actually exists in the soul, specifically, in the mind and emotions. The word of God teaches us that man is a tri-part being.

Most of us mainly relate to the physical aspect which is one part. The emotional, mental inner part of man is called the personality (part of the soul, the second part).

While these are the "parts of man" that identify with objects in this world (again, the five senses), it is only two-thirds of who we are.

If we want to understand physical or mental/emotional truths in our world, we consult our senses.

If we are to understand spiritual truths, we have to be open to the revelation of the word of God through our third part, our "spirit".

"If you declare with your mouth, Jesus is Lord, and believe in your heart that God raised him from the dead, you will be saved." Romans 10:9. This is a "spiritual truth".

Once we invite Jesus Christ into our lives as our personal savior, we receive His Spirit. We become one with him. Our spirit immediately becomes as perfect and complete as Jesus is.

Romans 8:11 says it this way." The same Spirit of God that raised Jesus from the dead now lives in you." (paraphrase)

Put simply, we are joined, now one Spirit with Christ. That also means man has the same Spirit guiding him that Jesus had.

"Herein is our love made perfect, that we may have boldness in the day of judgment: because as He is, so are we in this world." 1 John 4:17

Therefore, if we are in the midst of a crisis or life-changing event, "Christ in us" will get us through.

If we believe in His word that's living in our new heart, we can overcome every attack.

Salvation is all about enjoying the good life that Jesus has freely given us.

The good news is Jesus hears us when we pray, and he does not leave us when we are experiencing a crisis. Maybe you don't feel like he's with you sometimes. Don't trust those "senses". It's not about a feeling.

Jesus said in Hebrews 13:5, "I will not in any way fail you nor give you up nor leave you without support. I will not in any degree leave you helpless, nor forsake you, nor let you down."

2nd Timothy 2:12 convinces us that God won't break His promise. That, even if we are faithless (do not believe and are untrue to His word), He won't deny us because He would deny Himself if He did. He won't deny Himself.

God always remains true and faithful to His word.

Jesus encouraged us in Romans 12:1-2 to renew our minds with what He has spoken and fulfilled concerning us.

In fact, Philemon 1:6 adds, "And I pray that the participation in and sharing of your faith may produce and promote full recognition and appreciation and understanding and precise knowledge of every good thing that is ours in Christ Jesus." (AMP)

In other words, every good thing is already on the inside of each believer through His Spirit, the Spirit of Christ (the Holy Spirit).

1 John 4:8 reminds us that God is love, and as a believer, a life full of positive emotions comes through His Spirit in you.

Chapter 10

It's a choice! You CHOOSE!

As mentioned in the scripture 1st Pet. 1:2-4, knowledge of God will give you access to His promises.

You have to go a step beyond your natural feelings if you desire to control your emotions. As we've discussed before, your natural body can experience depression, anger, grief, bitterness, guilt, and many other negative emotions. While at the same time possessing God's love, joy, and peace in your spirit.

That experience is all in the soul of man. The reason is that it may be true that you are caring for a loved one whom the doctor says is dying, or attending a funeral of a child, or even having so much pain due to a broken heart that can make you feel like you can never overcome it.

Positive thoughts bring healing.

Thoughts you allow to go deep into your heart can either kill or heal you.

In other words, be careful about attaching significance to those thoughts.

Trials will come, such as, "Didn't the doctor just tell you that you have cancer? You should be worried."

Don't judge yourself based on that thought because it did not come from God.

Matthew 6:25 says to take no thought for your life. Do not worry. Worry will not change anything.

According to the scripture, everything that God has provided for us in His word is based on fact.

Christ died for our sins. FACT.

He was buried, and He rose from the dead on the third day. FACT.

In other words, we don't base what we believe on how we feel. If it were, we would all be living a life of inconsistency and instability, and both are curses, nailed to the cross with Jesus when He died before rising again.

Galatians 3:13 tells us that, "Christ has redeemed us from the curse of the law, being made a curse for us: for it is written, cursed is every one that hanged on a tree."

One way to overcome is to speak to your heart. Know that it is not the Lord's will for you to be emotionally destroyed. Know that God is not the one who makes people depressed, discouraged, angry, bitter.

You don't have to bear a cross or suffer for Jesus. That's definitely the way Satan does things, but not God's way.

James 1:13 mentions, "Let no man say when he is tempted, I am tempted of God:

for God cannot be tempted with evil, neither tempted he any man."

"Be careful for nothing, but in everything by prayers and supplications with thanksgiving, let your requests be made known unto God. And the peace of God, which passes all understanding, shall keep your hearts and minds through Christ Jesus." Philippians 4:6-7

In other words, what God has spoken through his word, He fulfills in our heart as we believe.

The real you (Spirit) only knows "love." God is love.

It is the love of God that sustains the believer as the heart is working through life-changing circumstances. To understand the real you, you must know and acknowledge what happened when you received salvation.

The enemy, "Satan," does not want a believer to know that we have benefits in the Kingdom of God. One of those benefits is God's unconditional love, a positive emotion.

Knowing love/Jesus will uproot all negative emotions that came through Adam when he separated from God due to sin.

Romans 12:2 explains how we should not be conformed to the world's way of thinking but instead be transformed by the words that Jesus has spoken.

We should also not conform to the world's way of doing things but be transformed by renewing our minds so we can prove what is good and acceptable unto God.

He desires to live His life through mankind... through you if you would allow Him.

If you have committed your life to Christ, you have a born-again spirit; therefore, your thinking now has to match your spirit. Reality tells us that we cannot see or touch our spirit. Your born-again spirit has no negative thoughts. Your born-again self experiences no pain. If you allow your born-again spirit to control your life, Satan would not be able to steal your joy.

Since we cannot see or touch our spirit, we need something else concrete and visible. For that, we have God's word.

To know God is to know His word. To know His word is to know His unconditional love.

Life-changing circumstances bring fear and discouragement. Its during these times that we should remember that God is always with us.

"It is the Lord who goes before you. He will be with you; he will not leave you or forsake you. Do not fear or be dismayed." Deuteronomy 31:8 (ESV)

"God himself said, "I will not in any way fail you nor give you up, nor leave you without support." Hebrews13:5 (AMP)

"...So we take comfort and are encouraged and confidently say, "The Lord is my Helper [in time of need], I will not be afraid. What will man do to me?" Hebrews 13:6 (AMP)

Jesus said, "I will not let you down."

With your confession of faith in what Jesus has spoken, you open the door for the love of God to rule in your life by faith. In other words, you have to trust what the word of God says happened in your spirits more than what happened in the natural man.

In the natural man are the problems of fear, frustration, stress, anger, despair, defeat, depression, etc.

Still, in your spirit, through your commitment to intimacy with God the good far outweighs negative feelings and emotions.

What God says is true; whether we feel good or bad. It's all about being established in the word of God in your heart. Inward thoughts can control your life now too, but in a positive way.

"You will guard him and keep him in perfect and constant peace all who trust in you. All whose thoughts are fixed on you." Isaiah 26:3

It is vital that we know what Christ did for us through his death and resurrection.

He gave up his life so that mankind would have access to a brand-new life.

It's called the great exchange. Jesus Christ took on man's pain and suffering in his own natural body by the Holy Spirit's anointing. The blessing is called love: His love only consists of positive emotions.

Isaiah 53:3-4 says it this way; "He is despised and rejected of men; a man of sorrows, and acquainted with grief and sickness:and like one from whom men hide their faces. He was despised, and we did not appreciate His worth or have any esteem for Him. Surely He has bore our griefs and carried our sorrows and pains."

In other words, He has experienced all pain. He is the only one who knows how we feel and is touched by our suffering.

"For we have not a high priest which cannot be touched with the feelings of our infirmities; but was in all points tempted like as we are yet without sin." Hebrews 4:15

Because of Jesus, believers are able to receive His righteousness and His salvation as a gift. That means our souls can agree with his healing that's already in our born-again spirits.

Jesus said, "These things I have spoken unto you, that in me ye shall have peace. In this world ye shall have tribulations: but be of good cheer; I have overcome the world." John 16:33

In conclusion, this does not mean that you will never experience another life-changing circumstance, but it does mean that you are never alone or without hope.

It does mean you can see things differently through the spirit's eyes by faith in the finished work of Christ because what Jesus has spoken; He has also fulfilled in YOU, the believer.

REFERENCES

Strong, *James Strong's Exhaustive Concordance of the Bible*

Comparative Study Bible KJV, Amplified, NIV, updated NASB

Dr. James Richard, *Grace the Power To Change*

Andrew Wommack, *Spirit, Soul, and Body*

About the Author

Pastor Melba Riley Boyd is a believer of Jesus Christ. Her belief and trust in the word of God has helped her gain personal success as a Pastor, a wife and a mother.

Married to Earle Boyd for 52 years, Melba has enjoyed her two children, four grandchildren and one great grandchild.

With degrees in Pastoral care and Social Work (LSW, MSW) for over 35 years, Melba has served as a Bereavement Coordinator and a Counselor. The Almighty God has given her tools that are effective and proven to bring victory to the lives of those in need.

Don't forget to sign up for the Midwest Creations Publishing Quarterly Newsletter on our website!
https://midwest-creations-publishing.square.site/

MWCP UPCOMING RELEASES AND AUTHOR LIST:

Adair Rowan
(Sci-Fi, Suspense, Science and Tech)

- Concentric Relations: Unknown Ties – March, 2019

Projects for **Adair**:

- Project Ariel

Chantay M. James
(Romance, Sci-Fi and Suspense)

Available to pick up your copy today:

- Valley of Decisions
- Waivering Minds, Book 1: Brainwaiver Series
- Waivering Lies, Book II: Brainwaiver Series

- ⬚ Brainwaiver Beginnings shorts: Wattpad (Chantay M. James)

Projects for **Chantay**:

- ⬚ Waiverings, Brainwaiver Series (Anthology includes novella 1.5 and 2.5).
- ⬚ Waivering Eyes, Book III: Brainwaiver Series (December, 2020)

<u>M. Renae</u>
(Christian Living, Marriage, Divorce and Family)

- ⬚ Allowed 2 Cheat: When Marriage Takes A Wrong Turn.
- ⬚ Allowed 2 Cheat: Study Guide
- ⬚ Allowed 2 Cheat: Workbook

<u>C. Marie Evans</u> (Black Romance and Action)

- ⬚ A Hater's Prayer (July 2019)

<u>C. M. James</u> (Nonfiction/Christian Living)

- Who Broke My Daughter's Alabaster Box?

Projects for **C. Marie Evans**:

- Annie B.'s Legacy (December 2020)
- Legally Bound (July 2021)
- C.J. Series – Action (2020/2021)
  - CJ Run
  - CJ Hide
  - CJ Fall
  - CJ Rise

Projects for **C. M. James**:

- He Still Breaks Chains: Quick-Hit Hard Truth Series, Book 2 (December 2020)
- Cracked Pot Communication for Fractured Folks: Quick-Hit Hard Truth Series, Book 3 (April, 2021)
- The Power of No: Quick-Hit Hard Truth Series, Book 4

Coming Soon:

Teresa Taylor-Williams
(Christian Living, Devotionals)

- Praises in a Pandemic: Overcoming Covid-19 (Devotional), December, 2021.

And many more authors are coming soon! Don't forget to check out the website for author swag, events and giveaways!

Stay tuned for bits and pieces of some of our publications!

Midwest Creations Presents…

<u>Author Chantay M. James and the Brainwaiver Universe!</u>

What if you could have anything you desire? Is what you desire worth everything you possess – including your soul?

Waivering Minds, Book I: Brainwaiver Series

Celine:

A Licensed Clinical Social Worker in Alton, Illinois, Celine Baltimore lives a content, peaceful life. Until one of her patients reveals that her sister has become a guinea pig for behavior modification technology known as "Brainwaiver," then disappears.

Left with a child's journal that paints her once comfortable life in horror and intrigue, Celine finds herself nose deep in corporate secrets, shifty attorneys and rugged, intense men (specifically Enoch Sampson or Sam for short).

Shocked that she's named a winner in the Brainwaiver contest (a contest she'd never entered) Celine learns of more missing children in Alton and their link to the hip new software trying to take over her life; including Sam's teenaged son.

An all-around goof that can't stop tripping over her Aubusson rug (or keep said rug straight) can Celine let go of playing it safe, fight the good fight of faith and get the guy in the end?

Sam:

A widower and ex-CIA agent turned owner of a family owned construction company, Sam picked up a few skills from his former life. Some he wishes he'd never learned. Espionage and secrets had been his business.

Missions and sacrifice had become his life. Growing cold again seemed inevitable... until he met goofy (and determined) Celine Baltimore.

Could he avoid that place of unfeeling and do the unthinkable? Retrieve his son and love again? Because protecting his family was the only thing that mattered to Sam.

It was something that he would do at any cost. It was more than a goal – it was a promise. And Sampson men ALWAYS kept their promises.

Waivering Lies, Book II: Brainwaiver Series

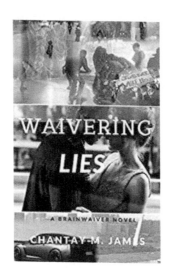

Max:

Max Arpaio is a Freelance Information Systems Security Analyst and part time Bounty Hunter on occasion. When Max responded to Enoch Sampson's call for help to find his missing son he realized something crucial.

The top government secrets and plots he'd stumbled upon long ago are no longer a shadow on the horizon.

And Now that Denise Ferry has taken up the gauntlet to wage a silent war against Brainwaiver, Max has to make a choice: To help the woman he loves but can never have or stand aside and watch as millions are led like sheep to a slaughter. Either way, he's a dead man. It's only a question of when.

Balboa:
Denise Ferry is a Business Consultant, former FBI agent and a severe pain in Max's rear. A woman who has gone from gang member lieutenant to military strategist to agent, she could write a book on espionage and silent war strategies.

So, when Denise engaged in a search and retrieve mission that targeted children for mind control experimentation, she's in for the long haul to wage war. However, she hadn't counted on warring on two fronts: Against the advances of Brainwaiver and to win the heart of Max Arpaio.

A man of mystery with a sense of doom, Max draws Denise despite her efforts to fight the attraction. Can she help him overcome his dark past?

As a strategist she realizes she has no choice.

Without him taking her back against Brainwaiver, she's already lost the war before she starts. And without him in her life she's already lost her heart.

Valley of Decisions: A Valley Series Novel by Chantay M. James

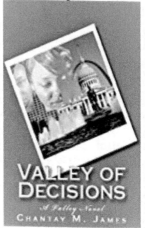

St. Louis, Missouri. Home of the missing.

Sandra Peters, editor for Re-born magazine, has planned her life to the smallest degree - her work, her friend, and her faith.

But when the prominent Christian magazine goes belly up and her friend attempts suicide, Sandra watches all of her plans crumble.

All she has left is her faith and her calling. For some reason, God has chosen her, a woman with an abusive past, to journey to St. Louis to save children. But how? And from what?

These questions plague the jaded young editor as she treks to find her destiny.

Little does she know that her war is not with flesh and blood. Little does she know that only self-sacrifice, unity, and love can defeat the evil that consumes the next generation.

Little does she know that, in the heart of St. Louis, lies her Valley of Decisions.

Author Adair Rowan presents the Concentric Relations Universe!

Concentric Relations: Unknown Ties

Psychotherapist Dr. Liam Ronaw enjoys a rather plush existence until new client's recite details about night terrors and dreams. Several dream descriptions spark a memory from his childhood. In an effort to help these clients, he follows the various clues as he works to figure out what connection they have to his own past.

Dr. Ronaw follows the breadcrumbs which lead him into a world involving a global coverup, a hidden community and a terrible new threat, the likes of which could spell doom for all life on earth.

Welcome to The Hater's Prayer Saga by author C. Marie Evans!

The Hater's Prayer

Naomi Carmichael Nee' Brooks was a Hater.

Well, a reformed hater, that is.
Destiny, her sister had been deemed by her church, family and all creation "the golden child," so Naomi knows how it feels intimately and repeatedly to have someone steal her thunder.

And now that she was about to be a divorced mother of three, struggling to make it on a state job, with an ex that was all about rubbing her nose in it, Naomi wouldn't know what to do if God hadn't given her what her and her bestie called, "the hater's prayer".

With a podcast that's growing by the hundreds, Naomi is sure that life was on the upturn. But she should have known better.

Falsely accused of hurting her kids, her ex-husband coming after everything she's got (which isn't much) and her (not really) hated sister sexually assaulted at a club; all while Victavious "Vic" Carter, the boy next door, has suddenly decided she's the one, can Naomi fully let go of her hater ways, trust God instead of herself, and give her old friend a chance to "shoot his shot?"

As a reformed hater, all by herself she doesn't have a chance. But with her bestie at her back and crazy family at her side, Naomi knows one thing to be true: With God, all things are possible. And seeing Vic through new and enlightened eyes, that may just include falling in love again.

Don't sleep on Allowed 2 Cheat: When Marriage Takes A Wrong Turn by Author M. Renae!

Allowed 2 Cheat: When Marriage Takes a Wrong Turn

I loved my husband. Looking back, maybe I loved him a little too much. Definitely more than I loved myself. How do I know? Because six weeks before our wedding I found out that there was another woman.

Devastated, I called him crying, trying to understand why. He explained that she started off as a friend because I made him give up his best friend (another woman and as such, a different story entirely, but really the same situation) to comfort me. He goes on to explain that it just turned into more than he expected and how he couldn't stop it since he didn't want to hurt her. He said that he did it to try and get it all (by all I assume "the cheating") out of his system so that he wouldn't cheat once we were married.

I knew then, in my heart, that his cheating would continue for a lifetime. But I was determined to keep the love I thought I found. I was so eager to hold on to that love that I told him, "I forgive you and we will get past this." Sadly, that wasn't the last time I spoke those words.

Throughout the course of our marriage, that refrain was repeated if not openly, silently... over and over again.

So, this is my story.

To protect those I love the most, I've changed names (including mine, just because) and the locations of various events. I also did this because the names are not important, neither are the places.

What holds true, or at least the truth that I'm trying to convey is illustrated in the message of this allegory. A message that so many women need to hear. A message outlined in the following fact that, as you read, you will feel this in your very soul:

BECAUSE I was aware of my husband's cheating during our engagement and set no boundaries or consequences; I gave him permission and consent to continue it during our marriage. I didn't walk away, and I should have. As a result, ten years later I'm still struggling with my sanity and choices.

Don't be me.

Allowed 2 Cheat: When Marriage Takes a Wrong Turn – Study Guide

This is the study guide to be read in accompaniment with the novel adapted memoir Allowed 2 Cheat, When Marriage Takes A Wrong Turn by M. Renae. (Memoir by M. Renae; Novel written and adapted from the memoir by Chantay M. Hadley and Midwest Creations Publishing).

Allowed 2 Cheat: When Marriage Takes a Wrong Turn – Workbook

  This is a companion workbook for Allowed 2 Cheat: When Marriage Takes A Wrong Turn (the memoir adapted novel as well as the study guide).

  Learn key skills that will assist you on your journey to healing from damaging relationships.

  With fun exercises and a journaling component built in, your quality time with God will take on a whole new meaning!

  Freedom, joy and emotional stability can be yours! Don't forget to pick up the novel and the study guide for a richer and more fulfilling experience.

Coming Soon:

Waiverings:
A Brainwaiver Anthology

Celine Baltimore and Sam (Enoch) Samson introduced the world to the Brainwaiver Universe in Waivering Minds, a place full of mysteries involving missing children, mysterious technology and race against time to save one from the other, never realizing that the target, in truth was Celine. And as mysteries often do, the saga didn't end with Celine and Sam...

Waivering Winds, Book 1.5:

Waivering Winds sheds light on the in-between-times, connecting Waivering Minds to book two of the Brainwaiver Series, Waivering Lies.

Delilah and KC's story.

As Celine's opposition, Delilah did her thing in Waivering Minds, but it wasn't all good... and surprisingly, it wasn't all bad either.

Learn about her horror story compiled of kidnapping, human trafficking and present day slavery. God and KC have their work cut out for them when it comes to winning Delilah's heart.

But neither one of them is about to give up. Read her story as God and KC show a woman hurting from the pain of her past that she is more than who she thought she was...

Waivering Times, Book 2.5

Novella 2.5 begins midway through Waivering Lies, Book two of the series.

Amanda and Cruz's Story.

Amanda, too young and too focused on saving the world from Brainwaiver (starting with her mom) finds Cruz irritating... and irresistible.

On a mission from God, Amanda is determined to win her war, and the man that makes her wish she never had to fight one.

However, Cruz Arpaio is no fool. Amanda, at nineteen, was too young for a US Marshall in his mid-twenties.

Not to mention that Denise "Balboa" Ferry-Arpaio, his new and military trained sister-in-law would kill him, if his brother Max didn't first.

So, Cruz left as he was told.

Years later, he still can't get the thought of Amanda Same out of his mind.

Determined to return for the woman he knows is his, Cruz never makes it to his destination.

What happens next turns the worlds of Amanda Same and Cruz Arpaio on its head; and kicks off the war that had been a long time coming.

Will Cruz and Amanda find each other again and somehow, reunite and reignite the powerful attraction that both of them can't forget in these Waivering Times?

Only God knows...

Made in the USA
Monee, IL
06 July 2021

73026311R00049